Catma

CATMA

Poems by

Gilbert Allen

Measure Press
Evansville, Indiana

Printed in the United States of America
First Edition

The text of this book is composed in Baskerville.
Composition by R.G.
Manufacturing by Ingram.
Cover Design: William Rogers
Cover Photograph: Cindy Rogers
Author Photograph: Barbara Allen

Allen, Gilbert
Catma / by Gilbert Allen. — 1st ed.

ISBN-13: 978-1-939574-05-3
ISBN-10: 1-939574-05-6
Library of Congress Control Number: 2013957220

Measure Press
526 S. Lincoln Park Dr.
Evansville, IN 47714
http://www.measurepress.com/measure/

Acknowledgments

The author wishes to thank the editors of the publications in which these poems have appeared, sometimes in slightly different form.

Able Muse: "The Mouse and the Mole," "Losing Containment"
Alkali Flats: "Again"
Appalachian Heritage: "Foreclosure"
Appalachian Journal: "Parade of Days"
The Centrifugal Eye: "The Prozac Poems"
The Chattahoochee Review: "Her Mother Explains"
The Cortland Review: "American Translation," "Postcard from Purgatorio," "And Now, a Word for Our Sponsor," "Rednecks and the Men Who Love Them," "In Praise of Lions"
Cumberland Poetry Review: "Holy Saturday," "Sinister," "The Ceiling without the Sun," "Catma"
Emrys Journal: "*Current — America, 2005*"
Florida Review: "Moonlighter"
Flyway: "Latecomer's Triolet"
Free Lunch: "My Guardian Biped"
The Georgia Review: "Ediots"
The James Dickey Newsletter: "The Lifestyle Resolution"
Kakalak: "Marriage," "The Dams and the Dikes," "*Vita Nuova*"
Measure: "Unmistakable," "Manners," "When I Heard the Learn'd Astronomer Correct a Student's Pronunciation," "Big Beautiful Rhododendron," "Pasture, with Daffodils," "Albino Rice at the Open Mic"
Mockingbird: "Independence Day"
New Verse News: "GROUND CHUCK $2.48 A POUND!"
Pembroke Magazine: "Way to Go, Gil!" "Context," "How to Make Love to a 50-Year-Old Man"
Poem: "The Woman Who Vacuums Her Driveway"
Poetry of the Golden Generation: "The Dr. Philanelle," "Reader Discretion Advised," "Stairways to Nowhere"
Poetrybay: "Lunch at the Park"

RE:AL: "Even As We Speak"
Sewanee Theological Review: "From an Athlete Dying Young"
South Carolina Review: "Tools"
South85: "Driving to the Blackberry Valley Transfer Station on Inauguration Day"
The Southern Poetry Anthology: "Late Garden," "Stairways to Nowhere"
The Southern Quarterly: "'Officials Are Optimistic He Has Been Killed,'" "The Dead of Summer"
The Southern Review: "The Story," "Daughter"
Swallow's Tale Magazine: "'A Poem Is, After All, a Redneck Entering'"
Theology, Vocation, Social Justice: "Academic"
Tipton Poetry Journal: "Inside Self-Storage"
Town Creek Poetry: "Saying Grace from One Horizon to the Other," "Two-Finger Exercise"
Troubadour: "A Toast for Closing Time, Thirty-Five Years Later"
The Uncommon Reader: "Reality's Turkey"
undefined magazine: "Rooting for the Redskins on Monday Night"
The Upstart Crow: "The Bard of Avon"
Wind: "Hooker Hokku"
Xavier Review: "Nobody's Tom"

For the Guardian Bipeds
(You know who you are)

CONTENTS

I. *Ediots*

II. *Marriage*

I. Ediots

My Guardian Biped

Absolutely no talking cats!
— submission guideline

Yes He can, yes He can,
He can open that can.
Open He can

most anything, even
His notsnout, even
this carpeted heaven

He stalks — like He's ready
to sprint up a tree
with pure *joie de vivre.*

But High Muckamuck
moves in slow motion — stuck
on two legs. The poor shmuck.

And His tongue couldn't tweeze
this Lilac Burmese
to pluck out the fleas.

Though it never unwraps
to sandpaper His lips,
it endlessly flaps.

Now He folds, in midair,
to conform to His Chair.
That stare. That stare.

He wants me, right there,
for a lap dance. Oh dear.
That hide with no fur

on One that can't purr.

Ediots

Too boring. Static. Why not crash the car?
Can you rite something less grammattical?
Americans don't speak pentameter!

Please try again. Something vehicular
and socially progressive would be swell.
Melodramatic! Why'd you crash the car?

We've no idea where your submissions are.
Perhaps you're being just a little *anal*?
Americans don't speak pentameter!

Keep writting! You'll get better! Presevere
and pleeeze subscribe! It's nothing personal,
but we luv action. Why not crash the car?

Who'd read this crap? Who do you think you are?
You sound just like a metronome from Hell.
Americans don't speak pentameter!

Your title's not a word. You've lost an R.
For God's sake, we don't publish villanelles!
Please do the world a favor. Crash your car.
Americans don't speak pentameter.

Her Mother Explains

When I held her gainst the television
nothin happened. I asked her if she felt
any better. *No* she said *Mama*
I feel the same. I didn't know what more
I could do her head's been hurtin her so.
But durin The Call The Cavalry they tell you
where the next Combination Miracle Service
and Holy Ghost Rally is goin to
be and it was here in Charlotte this week.
So I took my little girl in the car
cross town just to see what would happen.
At first I felt silly for even goin
for me believin he could help at all
then for not believin and still bein
there. It was real interestin I tell
you. *You drug addicts you alcoholics*
wreckin your lives — come on up to Jesus.

I wasn't sure I'd get another chance.
Just the three of us stood up there. And he
touched her. For nothin. I didn't pay him
nothin. *Ah-Hee-Ill-Ah* he said. He pushed
her head real hard with the heel of his right
hand right where she said it always hurt and
the doctors couldn't do a thing for her.
Come on Jesus. Come on in sweet Jesus.
And she felt better. My little girl said so
right there. He fessed to me he didn't do

it Jesus did it. But I don't believe
him. He did it.

The Dr. Philanelle

The world needs a remote with better aim,
I think. Madonna. Curveball. Mini-Me.
Beware of people who have just one name.

You don't break habits, This One now proclaims.
You switch them out for others. Like TV.
The world could use remotes with better aim.

I'd like to make a modest counter-claim:
Some thoughts are not fashion accessories.
Beware of doctors who just have first names.

But still, it's great TV. Tears without shame.
Contrition between ads for SUVs.
The world's remote. And, with no better aim,

life's often worse. I guess I'd be to blame
for Trey, Liz, Bryce — off-camera, running free.
Beware dope addicts who don't give last names.

I'll watch awhile, and see who Phil can maim
next. *Need to change?* Words just for you and me.
The world needs a remote with better aim.
Beware of oracles with just one name.

Unmistakable

WOMAN IN IOWA TATTOOS HER LAST WISHES ON HER CHEST
— newspaper headline

The man above her whispers, "Let's just wait,"
until she yanks her blouse up to her chin.
Her chest proclaims DO NOT RESUSCITATE.

He rubs his eyes, makes sure they're accurate.
He's seen lots of tattoos, but not this one.
The man above her whispers, "Let's just wait."

He understands. She doesn't want to date.
Her last husband got underneath her skin.
Her heart proclaims DO NOT RESUSCITATE.

They're in the backroom of the bar. It's late,
she's drunk. "You gotta *Harley-Davidson*?"
The man above her whispers, "Let's just wait."

She waits until he goes to urinate,
then grabs his keys. In the October wind,
her chest proclaims DO NOT RESUSCITATE.

Defibrillator paddles hesitate.
The ER nurses call the doctor in.
This man above her whispers, "Let's just wait."
Her chest proclaims DO NOT RESUSCITATE.

Inside Self-Storage

People come to us during different events in their lives.
— Stephen Benson, President,
Morningstar Mini-Storage

Say you've been told
sorry, corporate downsizing
is nothing personal.
Say your double-aught Infiniti
just killed somebody
whose blood you don't want
to wash off the bumper
for sentimental reasons.
Say there's a little blow
behind the horn.
Say your son has just taken
up the trumpet, vowing
to practice twelve hours a night
forever. Say you might have been caught
between a big house
and the big house.
Say, while you're staring
at your hand in a motel
or in solitary
at 3:30 A.M. on Thanksgiving,
you just want to know
everything inside your real life
is still secure.

The Lifestyle Resolution

affirming the heterosexual norm, approved prior to the IOC Torch Relay, bound for the XXVI Olympiad, Atlanta

Flames that no faggot feeds, nor steel
has lit. Did Georgie Yeats
have visions of *The Greenville News*?
Here, County Council's straights

have narrowed — no cathedral gong
for these Olympic Games.
Burn family values for a torch?
No faggots — or no flames!

No way! *Selah.* The IOC
need to get through, won't come
on foot, on principle. They rent
a van, a Dodge Condom,

steal down I-85,
flame into Georgia. Alive.

“Officials Are Optimistic He Has Been Killed”

— Radio news report, after a surgical strike in northwestern Pakistan

Driving, I barely hear — because
on Route 291,
beside the Greenville cemetery,
this afternoon’s big wind

has filled the world before my eyes
with real plastic roses.
A winter garden? Lost parade?
Whatever one supposes,

I guess — gas on tires, tires
over the rainbow roil
of slick colors, on striped asphalt.
Oil on oil on oil

on oil. It used to be
alive. This potpourri.

GROUND CHUCK $2.48 A POUND!

The flyer adds, SUPPORT OUR TROOPS
beneath our future burgers. Oops.

Publicans (Republicans?)
pour forth those endless Yes They Cans

while never asking why we should
hold privates' blood a public good.

Support our troops! It's always plural.
Imagine Chuck's a Cub Scout. War will

dog his troop from Boy to Eagle
till his Marine enlistment's legal.

Tip of our country's sword! Fantastic!
He'll serve us, till he's sheathed in plastic.

Chuck has no special interest group.
Be singular. Support a troop.

Manners

Politeness is organized indifference.
— Paul Valéry

I beg to differ. At the Cracker Barrel
a screaming, nearly ultrasonic boy
squirms at the neighboring table with his mom,
but I don't complain. It's not because

I'm indifferent, or deaf, or even
particularly organized, but because
I recognize, even respect, the limits
of morally acceptable constraints.

She'd have to kill the kid to shut him up.
But at the tennis backboard, rehabbing
my wrist, I hear a spray-tanned woman yell
"You winning?" over and over, till I politely

answer, "I'm just attempting to amuse
myself." "You must be easily amused."
She blasts her horn during my service toss,
then leaves half of her tires on the asphalt.

By any means, I'm not indifferent to her
or even to her Maserati coupe.
I'll dream of keying EASILY AMUSED
upon *Valerie*'s personalized door.

I won't, of course. That's what manners are for —
to keep us safe from the deserving rich

and their good lawyers, safe as we can be,
from Valéry or his emended bitch.

Academic

We all know what it means.
Even the sportscasters,
when the Ultimate Bowl
is so decided, so
lopsided they can't lie

to keep their audience
from refrigerators
or the remote control
any longer, cry *Now*
it's academic. Sigh.

Holy Saturday

for Duncan McArthur

Sunday we'll need to say nothing
and Friday left nothing to say.
What better time to grade papers
than Holy Saturday?

Between what the week did to Jesus
and what Yahweh did to the snakes
our credo's *Christo et Doctrinae* —
or, Mercy Upon Their Mistakes!

Behind the rocks of our desks
scrawling what passes for praise
we trust in the resurrection
if not in a decent raise.

When I Heard the Learn'd Astronomer Correct a Student's Pronunciation

for Carl Sagan, 1934-96

He laughed, "No, no. It's not *Your Anus*.
That planet's name is *Urinous*."
I almost asked him how he knew
His Cosmic Number One from Two.

The Story

for Jim McConkey, who had to read it

I was 19, maybe 20, walking
across Triphammer Bridge, new manuscript
in hand, when I tripped — and a sudden gust
carried the Corrasable Bond between
the guardrails, into the open air. I got up
just in time to watch those pages flutter
a hundred feet, to decorate Fall Creek.
No other copy, and no staircase down.

What would Ernest Hemingway do now?

I asked myself. Once on the other side
my sneakers backed me down from stone to slippery
stone, moist autumn shale, shellacked with leaves,
through a semi-vertical scrub forest
until I saw that metal bridge, now from
the bottom of the gorge. Amazingly
the pages lay like giant handkerchiefs
scattered on either bank, six on a side,
none in the rheum shed by the waterfall.
All legible. I put them back in order,
then looked up for the way.

I couldn't find
the almost-path I'd taken, so I chose
the easiest from where I stood. Halfway,
it turned into something harder, almost sheer,
next to impossible. I thought of turning

around, looked back with just my eyes — and felt
my feet give way.

Then I saw everything,
two things: a solid sapling on my left
and a spindlier one, off to my right,
with half its roots exposed above the rocks.
But those pages were cradled in my left arm.

I didn't think, I didn't hesitate,
I grabbed that naked, unsuspecting twig
with only my right hand.

By God, it held
and so did I. Rebalanced, on a ledge,
hands shaking with what could have been the cold,
I slid those pages underneath my shirt
next to my undershirt, to keep them safer.

These days, of course, it never could've happened.
We back up everything. That story would've been
safely on a hard drive, CD-ROM,
the manuscript disposable confetti.
I'd've cursed, then laughed, and then consoled myself.
At least paper's biodegradable.

Yet forty years later, it amazes me
that I could've thought — no, *felt* — within
my deepest being, that those words (my words!)
were worth my present and my future life.
The story? I can't recall even its title,
try as I might, or a single character.

It was twelve pages, pitifully unique,
I probably destroyed in shame or grief
a few years later. At best, I tossed them out
with reams of others, when I moved to where
I'm living now — a mountain where words matter
but not so much.

Moonlighter

That's what / Experts are for . . .
— Howard Nemerov, "Learning by Doing"

Reaching for my garage-door opener,
I see him swinging from a rope looped over
the top of a live pine, cutting the trunk
of a dead one into pieces that (once split)
would fit my tiny fireplace. He cuts,
shoves and swings, cuts, shoves and swings, and fells
them into a heap between an azalea bed
and a dogwood, both ready to blossom,
neither one losing even a swollen bud.

He must be forty feet above the ground.

Since I've been indoors, marking themes all day,
I can't help staring through my open sunroof
at this Flaubert in dungarees, dropping
logs like useless commas. Mesmerized,
I almost smash the bumper of his truck.
"Be careful!" he yells. "I got my dawgs in there!"

He likes to hunt when he's not moonlighting.
(His real job's with the power company,
riding the cherrypicker 8 to 4.)
It's his third day working, after work,
cleaning old chaos from a good ice storm.
He warned me Monday night about the widow-
maker — the poplar hung between the sweetgum
and the sassafras. When he appraised

things, he promised to fell it first, and did.
He climbed the trees beside it, trussed it up,
and anchored the rope's loose end back on the ground.
His first cut, waist-high, metamorphosed it
into a rough unsharpened giant pencil.
He trimmed it sixteen inches at a time
until only the slack rope was left.
And when I walked up to congratulate
him on his ingenuity, he stopped me
with a whistle — the splintered branch pointed
at my eye. "Your wife don't need no pirate."

So now I'm on the observation deck
with both eyes safely peeled. Beard streaked with chain oil,
saw dangling from his belt, gray bar trailing
behind him, he could be a hyperactive
squirrel auditioning for Yggdrasil.
The logs are thudding to the ground again.

When I've been blind for fifteen minutes, he lowers
himself to the lawn, finished for the night.

On the concrete, he could be Chuck Norris
wearing a baseball cap, surrounded by
an arsenal of saws. He files each one,
bracing it up in turn between his knees,
until I come from inside with his check.
He doesn't look — it's not my honesty
that's got him worried. "I don't want you cuttin
anythin I forgot. You call me back."

Either he trusts me, or he just can't read.
Before he leaves, I ask him to inspect

a loblolly too close to the garage.
There's no moonlight. He feels its bark like braille
and says, "This tree" — he spits for punctuation —
"ain't gonna fall nowhere."
                                        "But if it did?"

He takes a breath and blows it through his teeth.
I know he can look up a live tree's limbs
and tell to the nearest foot where it would land
if the ice got thick enough. He reads gravity
the way I read a poem by Ezra Pound —
not with affection, but with a grim respect
for the damage it could inflict on ignorance.

He circles the loblolly three more times,
then points across the driveway, safely. "There."

He loads his saws and slowly drives away,
leaving me with my now-emended yard.
One less problem to worry about, I guess.
I've asked him what the damn thing really means,
and he's been kind enough to speak the word,
without digressions on stupidity
or gross lacunae in my basic skills.

I'll bet he's bitching to his dogs right now.

Even As We Speak

for Chris Douglas

The clouds are gathering
overhead, like a worst-
case scenario, and soon
it will start
to cliché.
Yes, Virginia, there is
a dark and stormy night
and we're all
in it together, home alone
with our own poor thoughts
which aren't our own
exactly, thank goodness, but rather
scrawny kittens who've adopted us
against our wishes, with nothing
more original to declare
than meow.

Still, they've passed
through customs, they've gotten
their shots, they belong
now, and we love them, really
we do, because
they've practiced that greatest
of all virtues — choosing
to be here
evening the odds
against them, against us.

American Translation

What is the sound
of one hand clapping?

The question follows him
into biofeedback, months
of manual training, until
with a single
snap of the wrist, he can produce
the requisite applause, like Superman
at a gay rights parade.

Now he does it whenever
he goes to lectures
on Kryptonite or Chaos Theory —
with his arms spread wide over the seats
alongside him —
beautiful as a hummingbird
slam-dunging the sidewalk.

Sometimes people even mistake him
for a poet
with only one name.

Context

Advocates of the women's liberation movement are presently sweeping the country.

In your timeless creative nonfiction, it'd be
an unbridled belly laugh
a braless *bon mot.*

But in a cheerleader's ass-backwards
paragraph, filled with subjects and verbs
that can't even cohabitate
much less agree,
it's a dropped bottom, billowing
on the fifty-yard line.

And, in a newspaper's smudged lines
of hasty prose, who knows?
It's all context
the pros and cons
prostitutes and jailbirds

singing their so-called convictions
on the beds they were made to lie in.

Browning's Dutch murdered his innocent wife.
Get with the pogrom.
This is going to hurt you
more than it does me.
Ladies, you're going to clean my clock.

Reader Discretion Advised

Beware. This is the last Forbidden Subject,
the unassimilable fiberglass.
Madness, asphyxiation, child neglect —
trifectas canonized to death. But this,

this — breakdown of decorum! I'm washing
my Corvette (Golden Anniversary
Edition), the car that passes understanding.
Scatter its pieces on the ground, and I

could no more engineer them back together
than you could resurrect a withered rose.
One clean door thunks, soon followed by the other.
Almost a closing couplet, I suppose.

Not wanting to sound Republican, or worse —
ah, what the hell. I'll say just what I mean.
If there's no place in verse, American verse,
for one ode to an elegant machine

that's made it to fifty, I'll air-dry on the road.
Zero-to-life is breathlessness enough
for me. Back to my prose garage, to hide.
And yes, I plan to turn the engine off.

The Prozac Poems

1. *Genesis*

Let's have a little illumination here.
Nothing too harsh
something California, you know?
Maybe like what they got
at that fern bar on Adams Street.
That'd be pretty good
dontcha think?

2. *Calvary*

Gee Dad, what's the big idea
of hanging me up here
all by myself?

3. *Lear*

Maybe, maybe, maybe, maybe, maybe.

4. *The Garden*

Annihilating all that's made
to a green (and white) thought
in a green (and white) shade.

5. *The Declaration of Independence*

See man, sometimes when human events
get together and relate, it becomes necessary
to forget about brand-name loyalties
and go generic.
Does that make any sense?

6. *Rip Van Winkle*

I can't sleep.

7. *No Second Troy*

My life had stood — a loaded Gonne —
In Taverns — till the Day
She saw my Pharmacopoeia —
And carried Me away —

8. *The Waste Land*

Oh to be in London
Now that April's there!

9. *Il Duce*

Rush Limbaugh.

10. *Howl*

I've seen guys with above-average IQs
who seemed to be emotionally challenged
hungry, upset, in what I believe
were only their boxer shorts
but hey, it happens.

Albino Rice at the Open Mic

for Notorious Dana G

Ima sage with some rage in my 14 gauge
Keepin time with my crime gon fill my page
Hadda ditcha bitch who did it to El Salvado
Who could shovel till she dont know what she grovelin fo
Hadda teach that leech betta button her lip
Now the only dress she got is her rejection slip
Im infernal Im The Colonel gon go too far
Put her ears on the cover of the *APR*

In my sestet now Im rested gon do you new
Grab the nighties of some whiteys at *The Yale Review*
New Haven New York turn yo head and cough
Checkin out yo little bookies fo I dust them off
All you Massas at *Parnassus* betta watch yo butts
Cause my exit wounds gon grease yo guts

"A Poem Is, After All, a Redneck Entering"

—from the transcript of a taped interview with a poet who said no such thing but now wishes that he had

A poem is, after all, a redneck entering
his pickup with a few
beers, then tossing the empties vaguely
behind him, in the direction of
the bed.

A poem is, after all, a redneck entering
his pickup, who couldn't resist
his allusions to Rilke.

A poem is, after all, a redneck entering
the latest figures into his
checkbook and finding they don't quite add
up, after that last date.

A poem is, after all, a redneck entering
(his shoes caked with raw manure)
the house of your reading
through the basement window.

A poem is, after all, a redneck entering
your living room, to make
a primitive gesture of greeting upon
your carpet.

A poem is, after all, a redneck entering
your dresser drawers, roughly fondling
your darkest secrets, in a way
only you will ever know.

II. Marriage

Rednecks and the Men Who Love Them

Somehow, they'd always escaped
my attention, cruising inside their pink
Blazers, broomsticks mounted firmly
on the back windows, ready to fly

off the handle. Double-parked, listening
to Rush Limbaugh on FM, they're inspired
to spit in French — while the men
who love them are still inside

the mall, desperately searching
for the new underwear
that will save their marriage.
On the way home they stop

at some vegetarian dive
to swill and snicker
at Frank Gifford's wife, up there
on the big screen, looking as if

she were still a player.
They boo the Little Dutch Boy
during the commercials, telling him
to keep that finger

right where it belongs.
Meanwhile, the men who love them
sit outside, fingering their boxer shorts
through the plastic wrappers, looking

over their shoulders, waiting
in broad daylight for something,
anything, to rise.

The Mouse and the Mole

Marriage has many pains, but celibacy has no pleasures.
— Samuel Johnson

"Though you live in a hole,"
said the mouse to the mole,
"I know I can teach you so much.
By my soul, by my soul,
I'm just out of control
when your forepaws and mine even brush."

"Though you live in a house,"
said the mole to the mouse,
"You will make me a very fine wife.
By my paws, by my claws,
by my tail and my jaws,
I won't leave you the rest of my life."

In June they were married —
unhurried, unharried —
with nocturnal friends gathered round.
The band played in tune
on a bright honeymoon.
Then they tried to find their common ground.

They went to the knoll
proudly picked by the mole
for his mouse, as their new home-to-be.
With his forepaws he dug
while she purchased the rug
and the drapes and the HDTV.

And they lived cheek to cheek
for a month and a week
in their Paradise under the ground.
But then it befell
(though it hurts me to tell)
that their lives, with their paws, came unwound.

"Though we live in a hole,"
said the mouse to the mole,
"there's no reason for this *I* can see.
Can't we live in a house?
Oh, my dear, lovely spouse,
any hole is a hovel to me."

With his back to his mouse
the mole said, "In a house
I'd be hungrier than in a jail.
I couldn't find bugs,
nor a spider and slugs —
I'd be constantly wringing my tail."

"Oh, that's very droll,"
said the mouse to the mole,
"but bugs live in floorboards and sills.
There are termites and fleas
and roaches and bees
and if you can't find them, *I* will.

"I don't mean to grouse
in — *your* home," said the mouse,
"but I won't live here one minute more.
There's dust in my dough,

in my skirt and trousseau,
and I can't get the dirt off the floor."

"If you don't like *our* house,"
said the mole to the mouse,
"then you'll have to find some other rodent.
My sweet, lovely spouse,
the life of a fieldmouse
was all (so you said) that you wanted."

"Oh you louse, oh you LOUSE!"
said the angry young mouse,
"you're as bad as those insects you eat!"
Her snout twitched her head
and her whiskers turned red
and she left in a blur of four feet.

Now sole in his hole
sits a lonely old mole
while his stomach and stubbornness grow.
He lowers his nose
till it touches his toes
and he doesn't know where he should go.

He has stuffed both his cheeks
thirty years (and two weeks)
in his Paradise under the ground.
And thus it befalls
that the dirt and four walls
of his home hold no strife, but no sound.

So he pouts there at night —
for she never does write

from her house so impeccably neat —
yet he treasures the loam
of his own catacomb
while she vacuums the dust from her street.

A Toast for Closing Time, Thirty-Five Years Later

The band's long gone — it's after the last dance.
The bartender won't serve another beer
once his rag's wiped the counter down. "Last chance!"
He offers all the losers one last leer.
Three-fourths of them are staring at the floor
between their legs. Nobody else would peek.
A few wag eyebrows, still trying to score
with any chick not patently a geek.
Good God! A thousand ships should flee each face
still left in here — each guy's so damned pathetic.
One manages to grab his crotch with grace,
just having learned Red Dog's a diuretic.
Yet praise the Lord of Toasts — don't harbor a
doubt — because here's where I met you, Barbara!

Marriage

requiring public promises
of one's intentions
to fulfill a private obligation
— Marianne Moore

This eternal absurdity,
this Tuxedo Junction welcoming
the world's slowest train,
this democracy of two distinct
peers (standing
or sitting), this court
of constant appeals,
this theater
of the absorbed, this
legislature with one house
divided against

itself, still stands —
at least sometimes.
So pardon these candidates
who've chosen each other
over infinite parole
and palaver, even if they've changed
their sorry cells every seven years,
even if they've changed what's left
of their sorry minds, for better
or for worse, or even
God forbid, for good.

Daughter

I carried you downstairs, into the car,
and drove your mother to the hospital —
your would-be mother, holding you inside her —
who would've died if you'd have lived a little

longer. We'd have named you for our mothers,
Cecilia and Marie, now vanished too.
What's in a name? Nothing, like a rose
whose scent of absence fills the coming snow.

What I remember: From the seventh floor
I stared at that white desert — till two drivers
oblivious to me and to each other
ominously approaching in reverse

crashed mid-aisle. Got out. What could they say?
They shook their heads, their hands. Drove on their way.

Big Beautiful Rhododendron

Our church delivered you, a potted psalm —
Come, ye children, hearken unto me —
to bless us after that first operation,
the one that should've helped us have some kids
some twenty years ago. My, how you've grown!
So full of pink explosions you could be
a prom queen gone postal. Or a paean
to a freckled perfection never born,
that never found you out for hide-and-seek.
A mime in emerald, a silent hymn
to what? A resurrection, or a death?
We're still not certain, when we face your music.
Our friends have kids in college, kids in jail.

When you think about it (if you could think,
as the wind shifts your attention round the yard),
each plant commemorates some operation,
death, affliction. My mother-in-law's English ivy
smuggled from Long Island in a carry-on —
a tangled Underground Railroad in reverse —
long before she couldn't find her name,
let alone the New York-Greenville flight.
She passed last Easter, wordless, in no pain.

Hydrangeas from my father, which now grow
in wilting distance of his scattered ashes.
The long-dead neighbors' pear tree. Shasta daisies
flowering longer than a friendship. An aunt's

chrysanthemums, untouched by insects and
unmoved by her lingering, cancerous end.
They came, we thanked, we planted — nice and deep,
to give the hillside roots, to save the soil.
My mother dug a ditch, *her* strategy,
a year before her body washed away.

Pick the hole that suits your temperament.

My post-modernist acquaintances tell me
I'm always telegraphing the sublime
turn — the one that says I'm hopelessly old-
fashioned — looking for consolation in
this mass, this mess of flowers and foliage,
whose only purpose is to have no purpose.

With due respect, fuck them. I'm fifty-odd
years old, a child of The Enlightenment
no matter what the wattage of these bulbs
beneath my knees and omnipresent trowel.
Big beautiful rhododendron, you're too big.
They're in your shadows now, and have to go.
Stray daffodils, or tulips? Irises?
I'll wave these dirty flags like homemade kites.
I'll take what I can find. I know my rights.

Pasture, with Daffodils

for Barbara

They wave, upright and venomous
in April, hissing
Please Wordsworth me.
Chipmunks and cows have brains enough
to let them be.

But we're another story. Dozens
maybe hundreds
we've propagated
and praised, calling their distant cousins
domesticated,

our perennial babies. Blooming
idiots,
we've made our beds
and kneel in them, forever weeding
whys from *whats*.

Late Garden

Long since cleared
and mulched with leaves
from Bradford pears,
the garden still grieves —

or seems to grieve
from our upstairs window
this Christmas Eve.
Why should sorrow

fill this fallow,
rain-soaked place
and time, to harrow
mere empty space?

Only to trace
right there, below,
on barren grace,
imagined snow.

How to Make Love to a 50-Year-Old Man

Do you want me to buy the book?
— a wife's inquiry

Once upon a time, he arose
at the crack of dawn.
Time, understandably jealous,
thumbtacked their bedsheets over
the east window, swearing off her twin sister

forever. This lasted, oh, thirty years

until the doorbell rang.
Dawn again, gone postal, mail-crazy from licking
all those commemorative stamps, with an invitation
from the AARP, too good
for him to refuse.

Time didn't stand still

very long. Dawn gave her
her own birthday card, in the shape
of a silvery mirror, and said *Sis*
I'll turn him to stone
You live happily ever after.

The three of them make quite a couple.

Losing Containment

Nature abhors a vacuum. So
does he — he's close enough
to godliness already. But
an ex-free safety's wife

needs some weakside help. He's man-on-
man with the washing machine
while she does briefs in Federal Court.
His toilets look pristine

as punchbowls. . . .Flushing, he turns blue
as Vanish. Five o'clock
and he's forgotten to wrap up
tackling Coquille St. Jacques!

She'll hyperventilate —
or swear he can't pee straight.

Vita Nuova

It's one of two industries that refers to its customers
as users, and the other one is in Colombia.
— Paul Saffo, Director,
Institute for the Future

After leaving the industry
he was born again, twice,
at The User Friendly Baptist Church
in Menlo Park, California, because
the user is always right.
But he was one sorry
son-of-a-use, demoted from digital
to analog, golden parachuted at twenty-eight
with nothing left to use.
He'd even tried *Our User*
That art in Heaven, hollow
be Thy Use. The next day?
The Apple made him do it.

He thought of going back
to school, but they were admitting
only users with the right test scores
just like the HMOs. So he took stock
of his options: Apply for Users'
Compensation? Cry and run home
to his user? He'd hang out
at the fern bars, trying to use
inconspicuously, search engining for
that special user, the one
who'd email *I want to use you*

forever, honey, till death
do us use — virtually female, always
employing the binary, technologically sweet.

He'd round up the usual
users, but it was always
the same, no use. *You break it*
you've bought it they'd all threaten
on the third date, handing him
an unused condom, as if his attachment
were the world's deadliest virus.
Maybe, he thought, pressing
the DOWN button on another strange, shuddering
elevator, he just used an interface
only a motherboard could love.

Postcard from Purgatorio

(hand-cancelled by WS and WBY)

One married his Moll,
one gilded his Gonne,
both determined to mug
Her imagination.

Two-Finger Exercise (Piano Bar)

Men with ring fingers longer than their index fingers
are prone to violence and aggression.

You've kissed my hand —
now I'd like to kiss yours.
Please understand.
You've kissed my hand,
and I'm not looking for a wedding band.
Put down that Coors.
You've kissed my hand.
Now I'd like to kiss yours.

Independence Day

Melanie's perched on his shoulders, sneakers crossed
over his chest. They've snuck between parked cars
on the parade route, trying to accost
first Babar, then the Biker Mice from Mars.

His wife is on vacation in Madrid
while her divorce comes through. She'll get the Labs
and "domicile," he'll get the truck and kid.
"Daddy, isn't that *our* street?" She grabs

his hair, pointing to North Hill, afraid
the smoke's from a familiar spot. Offhand
he'd guess the hook-and-ladder's on parade,
trapped between the floats and marching band.

You can't beat home sweet hell for holidays!
Too bad their house insurance lapsed in May.

The Dams and the Dikes

The dams are good, the dams are fair —
they power the electric chair.

Dikes are ugly, dikes are squat.
Dikes are everything you're not.

Dikes are barren, dikes are glum —
they grab Dutch children by the thumb.

The dikes are clad in only dirt.
The dams have spotless concrete skirts.

Our dams are Detroit's biggest fans,
stuffing their kids in minivans.

Dams are California givers,
draining Colorado Rivers.

While dams endure their traffic jams,
dikes protect their Amsterdams.

Dams still worship our Prime Movers —
Herbert and J. Edgar Hoover.

The dams are grand, but somewhat vain —
they reap their profits from the rain.

Dikes, ecologically sound,
just take what they were given — ground.

Dikes don't pander to the masses.
Dikes don't make more greenhouse gasses.

Dikes are hermeneutic leaders.
Dikes are more than merely breeders.

Broken water's so pathetic.
Why can't dams be more — hermetic?

The Bard of Avon

Her customers are nothing like the sun.
Each day, she misses her concordance more.
O bloody period! Her life's a pun,
hauling her soggy ass from door to door.

She liberates her latest sample cases
so their eternal summers shall not fade.
She'll be the lord and steward of their faces
until her last tuition loan's repaid.

Allow not nature more than nature needs,
she tells the trophy wives, *and life's a bitch.*
Lilies that fester do smell worse than weeds —
he won't sniff dandelions in a ditch.

She hopes divinity rough-hews her end
because she has her thesis to defend.

Hooker Hokku

God O God O God
Ogodogodogodo
Godo good good GOD

Rooting for the Redskins on Monday Night

May God us keep
From single vision & Newton's sleep!
— for Magdalena Zaborowska,
a recent arrival

Unlike you
we're just here — a perfect example
of Blake's nightmare, scarfing
Fig Newtons before nodding
off in the La-Z-Boy
so to see the Cowboys get killed, we'll check
the smoke signals in the morning paper.

We're Americans, pure
and unhyphenated, though we suspect
our Great-Great Grandpa Genes
came from somewhere, sometime.
What we have as our better half
is this nothing inside us
never to be known.

How different it must be
to hear that other
vacuuming the house
of your heart, even if
you can't marry him
or her
or divorce.

How unlike this cartoon desert
island, with only the palmetto
of a single aerial
for company, surrounded
by endless waves
of infinite channels, which beckon
equally, from all directions.

III. Catma

From an Athlete Dying Young

We all are. Well, except perhaps
for those extraordinary chaps
whose hearts implode at ninety-one
beholding their first hole-in-one.

As for the rest of us, we die
in rehab or in surgery:
our bodies broken, our mind bent
on misconstruing what they meant.

"The best thing is to play and win,"
said Bobby Riggs to Billie Jean.
His 55-year-old Good News?
"The next best thing's to play and lose."

Track or diamond, field or court,
our time there is, alas, too short.
Raise? We can't even don the cup.
And then, at last, we just give up.

But dying once opens the eyes
to earth's impending, dark surprise:
that Lord of Flies, that Final Buzzer
after which there is no other.

Way to Go, Gil!

Born, you go about your business
in diapers, in bathrooms, then
at parties of the first party,
blundering from birthday
to birthday — a piñata
of Wal-Mart figurines
trying to be Venus de Milo
trying to bust yourself up
into beauty

paying an arm and a leg
for the big ticket item
that never works.

A Coupe DeVille?
Hell on wheels.
A pew?
Godsty.
What *is* the sound
of one check cashing?

Never enough.

That's why I'm here, mooning
the stars and whatever else
won't listen. Tomorrow
I'll be in the churchyard
playing softball, hitting home runs
into the cemetery.

Again

An apple is the earth
it grows on, first full
of itself, a perfect
round, then
reddened by its own
riches till it
falls, entering
the earth as part, as partner
in crime, vanishing
into the new
tree, the new
apple, which is the whole
sweet hopeful, sweet
hopeless earth again.

Latecomers' Triolet

after Copland, after Billy, after Lewis & Clark

Still grasses, dawn,
the open prairie before us.
Grays color from the cymbal of the sun.
Still grasses. Dawn
winter wheat, in rows, now gilded to explain
why birds cast open syllables of loss.
Still grasses. Dawn.
The open prairie. Before us.

Driving to the Blackberry Valley Transfer Station on Inauguration Day

Greenville, South Carolina, January 20, 2009

Maybe a seven-minute ride. Turns out
a lot of us white guys are here today,
pickups mostly, stuck with American flags
like Band-Aids over bumpers, back windows,
in honor of the history behind us.

Hauling two months of litter and beer bottles
from my blue luxury sedan, I must
appear to be a lost investment banker
hiding the bender he's still getting over.
The guy beneath the HERITAGE NOT HATE
cap smiles. "Looks like you had yourself a time."

He smells like he's biodegradable.
I toss Buds into the dumpster, one by one,
so he'll gimp off before my box is empty.

It works. It's only me, as I repop
my trunk, and drag bag to the garbage bays
to fortify the artificial hill.
Mission Accomplished. Although I'll be back,
sooner or later, with another load
of crap my cat and I want to be rid of,
filling what cavities our land still holds.

In Praise of Lions

King of Beasts? My ass. Singular,
plural, they beat up on
lost babies and the straggling sick.
A Young Republican

of Kenya *does* spare the unborn,
whom she adores, but taste-
fully, without demonstrations,
regarding words a waste

of the grace before which all else
vanishes, like self-doubt.
Why apostrophize your future
blessings? Prides go about

their business. Lions purr
I love you, raw as you are.

Current — America, 2005

after the painting by Katherine Porter

A memory of towers, melting
girders, kaleidoscopic oil
on canvas (a blue desert) making
a broken rollercoaster, hell
bent on treasure, big X marking
the heart of an amusement park —
while on the right
something white
as a weapon, missing a wing
or a trigger, aims at the dark.

And Now, a Word for Our Sponsor

In the beginning was the Word . . . .
Or at least it will be
in the end
when the waves of our pitiful logos, already leaked
to the heavens, returning
to You or Your empty
houseboat, raise
a music of our sphere

long after it has
vanished, a counterpoint
finally measured and priceless because
its black surf
in every channel
is all that is.

Lunch at the Park

She could be at McDonald's, grazing. Odd.
But the unicyclist is praising God.

Both arms straight up, surrendered to September,
this blissful woman is amazing! God!

A six-year-old squirts her with his Mac-10.
The unicyclist still is praising God.

She wobbles patterns in the parking lot,
her Alphas and Omegas tracing God.

No Manichean bicycle, no trike
for her! Just One True Wheel, begracing God.

With her free hands, she balances all praise,
blessing three Clemson fans abasing God.

They snicker, shout "Raise *your* hands if you're Sure!
Hey, honey! Who you think you're racing? God?"

Her Walkman isn't tuned to their Big Game.
No touchdowns fill her ears, dispraising God.

In self-defense, she turns her volume up.
She's listening to a CD raising God.

And here's her extra point, which no one hears
but me: *I've turned my other cheeks — amazing God!*

The Dead of Summer

Carolina coziness hits you
upside the head. All July
we stare through double-pane
tinted glass, shiver deliciously
in conditioned air, and behold

the dead of summer: lawns
blanching beneath
the high sun, shadows
nearly disappearing at noon, leaves drooping
everywhere, like they've finally run out

of antidepressants — ready for the big
jump. Underfoot at dusk,
they're an outtake from
a Rice Krispies commercial
as we guzzle sweet tea

ice crackling harmony
till it diminuendos to dilution.
The bricks on the west side
of the house could still give our fingers
the first degree. The black driveway

could still give a baleful voice
to bare feet. The stolid horizon still
whispers, in its hideous accent,
I'll be back.
But the night

beckons, a velvet masterpiece
abandoned on the side of the road.
It draws us to the sundeck,
blissful, without sun, while we watch the cat
play with something, till it stops.

Saying Grace from One Horizon to the Other

Marmalade from the same
jar, smeared
on the very face of God.

So far, so good.

Not a patient etherized
upon a table, or a wound
that bleeds afresh.

No, let us give thanks

for the Terrible Two, the kid
in His insatiable, sloppy
joy, doing big things
that take your breath
away — one way
or the other.

Dawn, dusk.
Dew, die.

And so shall
His creatures.

Now shut up
and eat.

Reality's Turkey

I speak, dripping, from beyond
the grave, a blathering
once filled with blood
now with stuffing.
You wish me to
disappear, and I do
in you.

Sinister

It's all about turning left

the NASCAR Living Legend declaims to the student
driver beside him in the hamburger commercial (too good
for me to remember which patty), flipping off high school
into a demolition derby headed for the takeout window, crumpling

every old lady's lemon into Flannery O'Connor's bitterest
truth: *nobody with a good car needs*
to be justified. Daytona 500s, velodromes,
quarter-mile cinder tracks — it's all sinister, fast

as we can go. Only the clock
has it wrong, goes right. For us, stopwatchers
all, backwards is the only way that'll ever help
make sense: riding the draft

of every ancestor, racing every race
in the opposite direction, swimming against
that smooth current of Jehovah's sweep second hand,
until, at the very end, we just hang on

for the hell of it, without helmets, and pray.

Nobody's Tom

How he got there
is a good mystery, but they know
he's behind the piano.

Maybe he slipped into the narthex
while the usher was outside
coveting a Cressida, or one
of the choir's children thought
he was cute enough to carry

or maybe he's always been harrowing
the boiler room, feasting
on scraps from weekly suppers
and occasional rats, and crazed
by Lent has taken the first
warm morning in April to come forth
for his communion.

Three of them manage to chase him
across the full table, but
he doesn't upset anything
and since Reverend Mike
isn't here yet, they can afford
to laugh as they shoo him over
the kneeling rail and out
the side door. Not finished, they gather

some extra bread from the sacristy
on an old salver and leave it
under the bottom step

where he isn't.
Here Kitty   *Here Kitty*
and they run through the graveyard to see
he's climbed the center cross
in the parking lot, surrounded
by flowering dogwoods, howling
as if he belonged there.

And when their fathers finally think
of driving their cars underneath
and honking, he doesn't even have the good sense
to back down.

Parade of Days

He's in his element, a perfect bed,
trying his level best to go to sleep
but not quite getting there. As usual,

he needs three tries to mouth The Lord's Prayer right,
attending to each word, flat on his back,
hands folded like a hopeful aerial.

So now it's time for this, his latest day,
to hobble after every blesséd other,
so many others, most beneath the ground . . . .

He always starts with names, then strains for faces,
correlating each to each — although
increasingly, he finds just photographs,

not images engraved upon his mind
alone. Those thought-prints? Faded into God
knows what, the anonymity of love . . . .

Their tortoiseshell is chasing a Rottweiler
up a tree, pinning its throat to a topmost
twig, triumphant — then falling through green leaves

into a drift of snow, her monument
a grave he dug — how many years ago?
Let everything turn into snow, he says

beneath his lips, within his vocal cords
half-tightening to each descending word.
Beyond the central air conditioning,

new snow lies on the drystack garden wall,
bearing the prints of other timeless cats
marching in time, between his countless feet. . . .

Awake, asleep, he moves to silent music.
He's new confetti on the mattresses
of Eden, full of himself in this parade

of days. Is every heartfelt goodnight kiss
the risen world? He'd like to think it so,
although his steps have melted into snow.

The woman on his left now vanishes.
He feels his steady breathing fall away
to somewhere words no longer have a place.

The Woman Who Vacuums Her Driveway

Sister of Sisyphus, she is always
there — sometimes at bottom,
umbilicus stretched to the source
of her power, her speechless, invisible
house that she would extend, far
into that other world.

And sometimes she's at the top, over
and done with, ready to roll up
inside — until she glances toward the street
and sees the finest dust
borne by the dawn breeze,
or by her own efforts,

she can never be certain.
So she reconsiders, covering
the same concrete she thinks
for the very last time — until
she stands in the gutter again
to look up, silently

at the hill that is herself

to say to all men and women
at wheel or window, more powerfully
than Rilke ever could,
you must change your life.

Tools

Under that blasted lightbulb he forgot
to replace, as his fingertips rummage
the toolbox for something stout enough

to pry the lid of the paint can
upstairs, he remembers
one of his mother's best mantras:

Never use a tool
for what
it wasn't intended.

And he wants to tell her
the man at Sears never slipped
the complimentary aluminum

opener into the bag, and even
her own son couldn't be expected
to own a crowbar *that* small

but she isn't listening.
So he takes the rustiest
screwdriver he's inherited and feels

for the first time her name
etched on its wooden handle
probably by a tenpenny nail

and smiles — and smiles again
when he knows just by opening
the past with this thing

in his hand, he's already
as guilty as she is.

Foreclosure

Who's repossessing the broke House of God?

Broke, not broken. It still lies, unfinished,
steel rafters piercing the unsteady sun,
rusting after a long, well-needed rain.
I figured it'd join the pantheon
of local eyesores: the fuel oil company
with ruptured tanks beneath its broken asphalt;
the Pharmacy That Never Was, smack dab
on Main — a merger-driven tax writeoff
worth far more as a fresco for graffiti
than as a retrofitted Dollar Store;
the textile mill that turned the river gold
or green, depending on the color of the day;
the tents the congregation used all summer.

It's like a skit on *Saturday Night Live*.
The minister, disgraced, got thrown in jail
for 5 to 10 — his favorite age group
as he so often noted on the flyers
he mashed in every mailbox within miles.

Yet someone saw an opportunity
to yank misfortune back into the black.
Today a truck, with Tyvek and a crew,
begins to put this Godsty in the dry.
What in the name of Christ will it become?
Too tall for mini-storage, and too narrow.

Too short for cell towers, and much too wide.
Perhaps an upscale vet? The HOUSE OF DOG,
making good use of the orphaned Portasign.

After the scandal hit the papers, where
did his entire congregation go?
Back to a smaller building, God knows where,
to piece together families, together?
To hunker up in mountain homes, alone?

Or did they scatter, wheat among our chaff,
to grow where chance and custom let them down?

The Ceiling without the Sun

for Claire Bateman

After the remodeling,
after the fixture's been taken down
and forgotten, after the sheetrock's been patched
and painted a perfect, unforgiving white,
he goes to bed, converted by mere happiness.

Only to awaken, on his sore right shoulder
in the newest center of night,
to gaze up, expecting
that misplaced metaphor.

And he sees, at the accustomed
angle, a lambency spread
out, unexplained by any window.

A streetlamp, through missing leaves?
Moonlight beyond?

He sleeps, safe in the diminished fact.

Catma

It's so much less
dogmatic, like
The Ten Suggestions
or Kittenchism.

No, it'll never swallow
that rednecked hummingbird
swilling flowers on Sundays, bestowing
the fruits of his fundament upon them.

It'll settle
for a simple cardinal.

Yes, the world needs
more catma, tails taken
to thinly robed hearts, till claws
tell us ENOUGH — and everybody

howls, getting his own hell
back to a corner of that rug
in front of the fireplace, cold
until Christmas. Let Patty Loveless

hold notes on country radio
like a beaten puppy.

Ma, you've been there
thirty-three years now.

Hold up your calico
and sing to God.

Stairways to Nowhere

for Bernard, Bennie Lee, Rudy, Jim, Louise,
Cecilia, Linda, and the rest

Once you live here long enough, you see
them everywhere. Today, for instance, driving
to the washerette (doing what's become
a weekly chore while we're remodeling
our laundry room), I passed the concrete steps
rising from a cracked sidewalk to only
a weedy field — a vacant lot between
the new library and the county park.
Within my memory, those steps led to
an elementary school my wife almost
taught in, job-hungry, in the '70s.
Before that? To the high school that preceded
the one now being torn down, across town,
for the new one — roughly halfway between.
More empty steps there soon. Which *there*, you ask?
Take your pick. It's only, as they say,
a matter of time. What every stairway says,
despite its length, or angle of ascent.

I load the washers, get back in the car
to take it for its weekly cleaning, too.
Air-drying, I'll recycle plastic bags,
aluminum, clear glass, and Styrofoam
my nagging conscience shoved into the trunk.

Why am I so compelled to rid myself
of almost everything? As if my life

itself were dirt, to wash into the void
from which the latest earth will soon return.
A cartoon from an old *New Yorker* pops
into my head: *Only what I need, O Lord,*
but make sure it's the highest quality.
You could do worse for articles of faith.
The washers stop when my (clean) car returns.

I've always been a sucker, I suppose,
for staircases. Our first remodeling
involved replacing a straight wooden one
with a black metal spiral — clockwise down.
Precisely the opposite, I learned, of Yeats's
tower, of the medieval preference —
counterclockwise, to let right-handed lords
use their dominant arms against intruders.
In nearly thirty years, we've never had
a break-in. Officially, the mountain ends
across the street, so we're the outliers.
Our terraced yard must be a burglar's nightmare —
pretty as hell, but even harder to
negotiate, especially in the dark.

But now is bright November sunshine, so
I'm hanging sheets and towels out on the line
in the backyard. Returning to the car
for the delicates, I'm struck by our front
entrance — with its landings, planters, leading
to the foyer, all redone ten years ago —
a young architect's *tour de force*. And I
recall the old brick stairs, marching straight up
the broiling western side of the house. The plan

was elegant, as mathematicians put it —
no steps had to be torn away. The old
served as substructure to the new. And as
I zigzag up, landing to landing, holding
empty laundry baskets, I remember
buried friends who walked those buried stairs.
Above, around, about, my dirty sneakers
hover. *We love, and love what vanishes.*
That's Yeats (misquoted). But for now, my feet
have the last word, for nowhere, and for once.

The Author

Gilbert Allen is the author of six collections of poetry: *In Everything*, *Second Chances*, *Commandments at Eleven*, *Driving to Distraction*, *Body Parts*, and *Catma*. He also edited the anthologies *45/96* and *A Millennial Sampler of South Carolina Poetry*. His work has received The Robert Penn Warren Prize in Poetry from *The Southern Review* and has been featured on *The Writer's Almanac* and *Verse Daily*. He is the Bennette E. Geer Professor of Literature at Furman University. Since 1977 he has lived in upstate South Carolina with his wife, Barbara — and with their eight unforgettable cats.

www.ingramcontent.com/pod-product-compliance
Lightning Source LLC
Chambersburg PA
CBHW020300030826
48979CB00026B/1660/J

* 9 7 8 1 9 3 9 5 7 4 0 5 3 *